Rediscovering America

Courses To Steer

GARRY HOYT

DEDICATION

To the men and women of our armed forces, whose presence and vigilance
preserves America's freedom and provides us with unique individual
opportunities to pursue excellence on our own terms.

CONTENTS

GARRY HOYT

FOREWORD

This is a short book, and deliberately so, because brevity recruits the proven strength of simplicity to the worthy cause of exposition. My years as a Creative Director in a large Advertising Agency instilled that skill, and a lifetime of sailing, including participation in two Olympics, reinforced the value of competition to enhance concentration. I have endeavored to combine these factors in a brisk review of the challenges facing America, land that I love.

Garry Hoyt

Chapter 1

Balance Fairness & Reality

There is an elemental tension between Fairness and Reality—they do not operate in natural harmony. The physical world of plants and animals, sea and sky, acts and reflexly reacts to realities. But the human world as it has progressed, has increasingly superimposed considerations of fairness onto the often harsh terms of reality. This is progress, and it could be said that the degree to which fairness has been successfully melded to the management of realities is the degree to which societies have become civilized. The difficulties come when fairness and reality get so out of step that the former trips on the latter. Non selective loyalty to the demands of fairness can quickly beget the neglect of reality with consequences that satisfy neither cause. This is a hard one to handle because fairness always presents itself so much better. A person who is fairer is better, and a society which is fairer is better. Unfortunately this focus on fairness does not always translate to better off in terms of the delicate linkage between economic progress, civic calm, social justice and spiritual satisfaction—the cornucopia that we have come to expect as our national due in America. And History is replete with costly instances of confusing attractive theory with rational fact.

The academic and intellectual worlds seem disoriented on this issue. Having traditionally and commendably led the quest for social enlightenment, they have tended towards vesting fairness with a royalty that too easily overrules reality. There is no better proof of this than Academia's long standing love affair with Socialism, an indiscriminate infatuation that never even bothered to touch base with reality. After years of costly experimentation it develops that Socialism is an inherently flawed system, now widely discredited for its basic unworkability and damaging side effects. Winston Churchill years ago described Capitalism as the unequal distribution of wealth—and Socialism as the equal distribution of poverty. In his more scathing complete quote Churchill said, "Socialism is a philosophy of failure, the creed of ignorance, and the gospel of envy, its inherent virtue is the equal sharing of misery." He had it dead right. But Socialism's smokescreen of better fairness enraptured intellectuals', and their approval encouraged an international illusion of legitimacy, the indulgence of which has led to a convulsion of impaired economies. Worst of all the imposition of Socialism's promised equalities required ever higher levels of government intrusion, often with collateral damages of cruelty and loss of personal freedom.

In retrospect it would be hard to conceive of a larger error of judgment and it came directly from those most presumed with better judgment. Yet many academic leaders have now jauntily careened from their classic miscalculations on Socialism to the almost equal foolishness of "politically correct" thinking. America has a right and a need for wiser ken than this. Whether I can do better or not remains to be seen, but it will be hard to do much worse. My hope for better luck lies in a different perspective—a viewpoint shaped by the sea.

All of us have had some dominant force which more than any other shapes the way we see things. For some it is parents, or schools, or religions or political doctrine. For me it was first and always the sea, alongside which, and on which I have lived all my life. It would be a stretch to say that the ocean is some sage purveyor of eternal truths. But the sea is definitely a kind of fluid lab that tests and impels people in ways quite different than the land. Survival at sea sharpens the senses in unusual ways. In sailing you must learn to simultaneously control two dynamic fluid mediums. First is the wind, a potentially destructive force often acting directly against you that must be aerodynamically bent to serve as a source of forward propulsion. Second is the water, a fluid some 600 times denser than air that supports you by flotation, but can also beat you back when whipped by the wind into opposing waves. Above all, the sea is a great "humbler," a dedicated reducer of cant and pretense.

4

There is nothing that man makes that the sea in its marshaled fury cannot break. The sea does this with absolute disregard for race, religion or economic station—it is if you will—the ultimate equal opportunity destroyer. No amount of posturing or wealth or moral superiority will buy you an ounce of extra tolerance from the sea. Carelessness is consistently punished, generally in fair proportion to the stupidity involved. Flurries of foolishness may temporarily flourish, but in prolonged phases it never prospers, and inevitably draws its pay in some degree of disaster.

So how is it that I, a sailboat designer from Newport, RI should presume to preach on this complex, arcane subject? Frankly I have been emboldened by my recently achieved 80 years—a station I like to think of as approaching the age of reason. I have no illusions about age being any automatic passport to wisdom, but age does serve admirably as a lens to sharpen one's focus. Suddenly the path ahead is markedly and irretrievably shorter than the road behind, and the realization dawns daily that there may be only yards to go before you sleep. This reality creates a concentration of thought hard to imagine at an earlier age—a hastened urge to get on with whatever it is you have to say—before the clouds move in.

So, well past the follies of youth, but not past the pleasure of recalling them, I feel empowered to inflict my ideas—if not on history—at least on pliant family and friends too polite to decline. As stated, I do this fully doubting that we get smarter as we get older—often quite the contrary. But we do gather with age a kind of cluttered savings account of proven mistakes, the awareness of which may marginally reduce the all too prevalent human capacity for damn foolishness.

Presumably that is why primitive tribes, who had to live closest to the fierce forces of nature, instinctively looked to graying elders for leadership—a guidance they felt justified by age as a badge of proof of having survived without catastrophic error. I know for example, that 70 years of sailing have taught me that safety at sea depends far more on *subtracting ordinary stupidities* than on *adding rare genius*. If you pay trained attention to the observable realities, God and Nature are generously there with the information necessary to steer correctly. The sea requires a prompting of boldness to be there, and persistent caution to remain there, and in the judicious balance of those elements lie some essentials we appear to have lost.

Above all, at sea there are clear lessons of cause and effect. Do *this* wrongly and you will get *that*, usually right in the face. Constant awareness of predictable and unpredictable consequence is at the heart of the sailor's art, and I hope to bring that nautical outlook to bear on some of our land lubberly logic that appears to have lost its bearings.

It is evident to me that America has of late been afflicted by a series of infectious delusions, which in there combined contagion threaten the well being of this fair land and its future citizens. A gradual enthronement of assorted absurdities has created flawed criteria to which America is now trying to perform, with frequent frustration. The nonsense is fairly evenly spread between the left and the right, and is the more virulent for that versatility.

I venture into these waters, normally reserved for politicians, professors and pundits, only because that group has so plainly botched the job. I do so unencumbered by any impressive academic credentials, and unpressured by any detectable public demand. My non scholarly view stands little chance of pleasing the intelligentsia, but that at the same time sets me blessedly free of any need to pander in that direction. Your reason to read could be summed up as the faint hope that this unsummoned view from an unexpected quarter might stir some of the fresh wind we need to fill America's sails once more. So, invoking some calypso wisdom, "let's hoist up the John B sail, and see how the mainsail sets."

Chapter 2

Improve the Creation and Distribution of Wealth

The very few reliable formulas that exist for the better *creation* of wealth are more than matched by the multiple schemes that have arisen for its better *distribution*. Most of these schemes have foundered on the reality that you cannot effectively *multiply* wealth when your driving force is a desire to better *divide* wealth. There is an inherent contradiction here because the latter goes against human nature and inevitably becomes a distraction and subtraction from the former. This contradiction illustrates the core contest between Capitalism and Socialism.

It is an observable fact that there is no more comfortable position from which to observe and criticize the many inequities of Capitalism, than from the wealth that Capitalism so uniquely provides. So the ultimate irony may be that Capitalism's demonstrably better power for the creation of wealth—most notably exemplified by America—is what provides the lasting lure for Socialism's better promise for the improved *distribution* of wealth. The central delusion of Socialism is to presume that Capitalism's better creation and continuance of wealth will still apply while imposing the governmental control necessary to assure Socialism's promise of better distribution. In real life applications, providing the governmental power necessary to make Socialism work automatically cripples and cancels the capitalistic capacity for generating wealth that forever tempts socialists. This is a self fulfilling formula for frustration.

Historically Socialism's higher minded promise of better wealth distribution makes it the not so secret sweetheart of the intellectual left and the academic and journalistic worlds. This support is often enough to provide protective cover for exploitive politicians who see more personal power in an unvoted, gradual shift from free enterprise to Socialism. That shift inevitably involves an ever increasing tax burden, which becomes a quicksand for Capitalism, and that in turn creates an ever increasing need for more corrective government stimulation. The very phrase "government stimulus" may be the quintessential oxymoron. Because if there is one thing government is demonstrably not suited for it is the stimulation of wealth, a field where their positive record is near zero and their negative effect legendary. The best that government can hope to do is to preside over policies that allow and encourage the vital freedom to create wealth, and to scrupulously avoid those policies that impede or unnecessarily complicate the creation of wealth.

Of course what makes redistribution of wealth so seductive to politicians is that the capitalistic extremes of wealth are conveniently concentrated, highly visible, widely envied and—most important, numerically insignificant from a voting point of view. This makes extremes of wealth a natural target and many would say—justifiably so. After all, millionaires obviously have plenty of money, far more than they need for their daily bread, and far more than the average hard pressed citizen whose far greater numbers make them a more decisive factor in any election. So if subtracting a little wealth from those who already have more than enough can be re-channeled to provide more welfare for the needy, and better healthcare for the general public, most Americans would probably say "let's do it." It is hard to argue with that, and even harder to win elections against that promise.

The problem is that the understandable envy and resentment of capitalistic wealth can be easily deviated to run down the slippery slope to Socialism. As an example, the recent financial implosions in the U.S. and Europe have raised new doubts about the basic soundness of our free enterprise financial systems, doubts that can quickly lead down the garden path to Socialism as a necessary correction to Capitalism's conspicuous failures.

Exacerbating all this is the unfortunate fact that we have allowed the mere manipulation of money to become one of the most highly rewarded capitalistic skills, and with that basic error the whole free enterprise structure gets warped and loses its restorative balance. Somewhere in the sacred screed of capitalistic virtues to be encouraged, we need to engrave the basic premise that the highest rank and reward should be reserved for those who *invent* things, or *make* things or *grow* things better.   Energy directed towards devising complex "derivatives" and other financial maneuvers is a deviation of free enterprise that should not qualify for either respect or reward.   Those practices are best described as ingenious mischief, the indulgence of which can only distract an economy from its more vital task of inventing, making or growing things.

The inherent natural strength of capitalistic free enterprise lies in its equal ability to promptly either *reward* success or conversely to *penalize* failure. Government bailouts, however well intentioned or popularly received, directly interfere with this balance. When your performance earns you the deserved right to fail, that right needs to be as zealously guarded as the right to succeed. That sounds brutal, but like the shock arrival of a large unwanted cold water wave, it serves admirably to alert you to the need to correct course. That awareness is the key to skillful steering, an art that seems critically absent in present day political jockeying.

GARRY HOYT

Chapter 3

Recognize Racial Differences

When we explore race relations in America we enter a separate land where nobody can say what they really think, and what is observably true is repeatedly discarded in favor of what we would prefer to be true. White guilt, Black indignation, and a democratic desire for equal results have taken charge and from these unassailable towers of higher intent, emotion holds sway over everything—including workable facts. Abandoned in the wake of this rush to righteousness are truth and candor, precisely the tools most needed for real solutions.

In this make believe world, where to call a spade a spade is as unacceptable a technique as it is a comment, the intellectuals and academics who should be leading the way in dispassionate analysis and advice have instead become the chief agents of obfuscation. Today there is no quicker path to academic Siberia than to be labeled racist—however spurious the charge or frivolous the evidence. The mere threat of having to even face a charge of racism would make any career concerned professor shake in his/her boots. So a strong sense of self preservation prevails at our colleges and universities, and any facts, opinions or behavior that might in any way be subject to the charge of racism, are simply avoided by general agreement. Fear of the bludgeon of the racist charge today chills college debate with the same intimidating effect as when Senator McCarthy once bashed people as he laid about him with the label of "Communist."

Being neither professor nor politician, perhaps I can approach this question openly, just as I see it. First off when we talk about "racial" problems, we most of the time mean Black problems. That admission is of course by itself a racist observation. But racial truths are not racist any more than medical truths. It happens to be

11

a medical fact that Blacks suffer some diseases more than whites, and vice versa. It is also a clearly observable truth that while other racial groups have difficulties in the USA, none have difficulties to the same degree that Blacks do, and the extreme problems of our Black population go way beyond their 12 percent share of our population. If we can't admit that reality, we can't begin to solve it. Blacks in the public mind have come to represent a microcosm of all that can go wrong in a society, because they hold a disproportionate lead in wide areas of National concern: crime, drugs, welfare, illegitimate births, low test scores and unemployment.

Recent statistics show 70 percent of all Black children now being born out of wedlock. This very tough statistic is the root cause of most Black problems. The difficulties may also begin with our terminology—we can't seem to settle on even a proper descriptive term. We have gone from Negro to Colored to Black to Black American to African American. Each change of terminology has been hailed as a description of greater accuracy and sensitivity, with very little discernible change in economic or attitudinal results. Our very process of classification is irrational. When a Black marries a White they together produce "Black" children—not White children. Is this lapse of logic because we feel Black genes are so much stronger than White that they dominate? Or do we feel Black contamination is such that any touch of the brush forever tars any child who happens to have an ounce of Black blood? Neither explanation makes much sense or justice. Even when a person can be visually identified by their light skin and non African features as having predominantly White ancestors, we—everybody—insists on labeling them "Black", which by everybody's admission is the category most prejudiced against. Should a person who by appearance is obviously 90 percent White and 10 percent Black presume to classify themselves as White, they earn the scorn of both races for trying to "pass" as White. This places a large number of very light tan people in a sort of no man's land where they are barred from acceptance as Whites, but also denied full credentials as Blacks. The many "Blacks" who are by genetic count as much White as Black, should be uniquely qualified to see both sides of the issue, but we insist on forcing them into the "problem" side with no recognition of their bi-partisan genes. We need the balance of this group and they should not be polarized by name tag classification into a stereotyped racial corner.

Even talking in terms of Black and White categories verbally slants the issue into the reflex contrast of polar opposites. In the color spectrum there is no greater contrast than that between the values of Black and White. Our accepted description of two sharply delineated points of view in an argument is to say that the issues are "Black and White". These linguistic labels pre-load the dice in an unnecessarily confrontational fashion. Since we seem addicted to the need to categorize people racially, we should officially open up the brown or tan category as being genetically and descriptively more accurate, and psychologically necessary to adding some new middle ground where better solutions might be found.

Of course everything is complicated by the historical and shameful fact of slavery. This has been distorted into a permanent excuse for underachievement by generations of Blacks who in no way suffered slavery, as well as a permanent source of blame for generations of Whites who in no way created it. While we have been able to put behind us our bitter and entirely justified enmity to the Germans, the Japanese and the Russians—somehow we cannot earn that kind of friendly truce with our own Black population. But for Blacks to hold this grudge, and to try to hold Whites to it, is a non-productive fixation that sets exactly the wrong tone. To suggest that, "We were sinned against, so you owe us" is simply not a winning strategy for anybody and certainly not for Blacks in America.

Add to this the three basic negative agitations that underlie and permeate every discussion of race in America:

1. Black people are at the bottom of the economic ladder.

2. Black people are near the top of the crime problem.

3. Black people are heavily involved in welfare.

Point number 1 is justifiably resented by the Black minority, and points number 2 and 3 are justifiably resented by the White majority. The Black population and supporting liberal elements see these three as interlinked events, directly deriving from White abuse, neglect and prejudice. The White majority views these events largely with fear, frustration and growing resentment. Drawing out the debate along these lines is leading us apart, not together.

What must be introduced into the equation are some progress factors which seldom achieve proper notice. America's record on race is certainly not perfect, but it is better than any major nation has ever done, anywhere. Second, there is, right now, a better life and more economic opportunity for Blacks in America than in any other country—including *all* of the African countries. No one wants to admit it—but nowhere in the world have large populations of Blacks ever done well economically, and the places they do worst are those where the population is almost exclusively Black—as Haiti tragically reminds us. Observing this does not relieve America of its duty to try to bring Black Americans up to better levels of economic benefit. But there are positive factors of forward motion that should be taken into consideration when judging the slow and erratic pace of progress. On race relations, most of America finds itself somewhere between the excessive self satisfaction of the right (we've already done too much) and the excessive self flagellation of the left (we haven't done nearly enough). Americans are generally willing to do more, but they are not satisfied with the remedial policies presently offered and they are growingly concerned about the cost and fairness of quotas, affirmative action, and "adjustment" programs. Mostly the White population seems puzzled and paralyzed by the gravity and persistence of the large national problems that result from the relatively small segment of our population that is Black. The legal hurdles to Black advancement have been cleared away, but the expected payoff of economic improvement has simply not happened.

Schools were rigorously de-segregated, even to the concocted contortion of forcing kids to be bussed across town and back. But the promised results of Black scholastic equality have not materialized. There is growing skepticism about what we may have gained, versus what we certainly lost, by driving our kids out of their neighborhood public schools. And when a White couple walks down a city street today and sees an approaching group of young Black males, the anxiety they feel is indeed racial—but it is no less real for that, and it happens to be based rather solidly on the uncomfortable fact that a high percent of the crime in the USA is currently committed by the low percent of our population that is Black. This is yet another example of a racial truth, the noting of which makes one a realist, not a racist.

It happens there are a number of unpalatable racial truths which by present day definition would be termed racist in tone or implication. This has had the effect of banishing a whole area of facts from polite conversation or public, political or academic discussion. But this artificial exclusion has in no way diminished the relevance of these truths as things that sooner or later have to be dealt with if real solutions are desired. Our unwillingness to admit to core problems has rendered us incapable of solving them.

Key amongst this group of unwelcome truths is the fact that Blacks as a group score poorly on the standard academic tests. It is no good blaming this on slavery—or on economic hardship—or on White prejudice. The Asians who now lead our academic parade, for the most part arrived here as destitute foreigners without even the advantage of speaking the language. Yet from this start, behind everybody else, they have generally achieved outstanding economic and academic success, without ever causing a significant crime or welfare program. A measure of Asian academic success is that a number of our universities now have to arbitrarily limit the number of Asians admitted, despite their superior test scores. Contrast this to the common college practice of forgiving low Black scores in order to achieve a satisfactory quota of Black students.

There are some racial injustices operating here that should be examined.

To the coolly objective eye, it should be no more remarkable that Blacks have observable difficulty reaching White or Asian educational standards than that Whites and Asians have observable difficulty reaching Black athletic standards. It is the frantic intellectual dance to avoid that simple admission which has thrown most of our remedial policies askew. We cannot properly address the problem because an over commitment to fairness makes us deny the very differences that create the problem. Thus, when Blacks on the average score lower on I.Q. and SAT tests—the tests themselves are blamed. The designers of tests find themselves besieged for change, forced into a search—not for tests that would better measure accomplishment—but for tests that will somehow deliver equal results to all races. Unequal results are taken as prima facie evidence of an unfair test. This does not stand to reason. It is as if one should ask to throw out the stop watches at track meets because they clearly record the fact that Blacks sprint faster than anybody else. At last count the top 50 sprinters in the world were Blacks from widely different cultures and countries. It is a virtual certainty that all the sprint medals and probably most of the finalists (male and female) in the next Olympics will be Black. The world records in all the sprint relays are held by all Black teams of runners. This cannot be explained away, as some have tried, by simply asserting that Blacks practice harder in athletics because other areas are blocked to them. It so happens that sprint speed is one area of athletics where practice is least decisive and where inborn, natural talent is dominant.

Unlike distance events where diligent practice can build endurance, no amount of dedicated practice can build championship sprint speed. It is something you are born with—either you have it or you don't. Overwhelmingly, Black runners have it and comparatively, White runners don't. Black athletic superiority goes well beyond sprint events in track, and includes virtually every sport where Blacks have been allowed to compete on an even basis. Our best athletes in football, basketball and baseball are Black. The domination of all major professional sports by superior Black athletes is now so well established that professional basketball is almost an all Black sport. A White wide receiver is not only a rarity—he may be an extinct species. The reality is—there is simply no White man around who can match the athletic skill of a Michael Jordan or a Carl Lewis. That is very tough news to a majority of White athletes who are doomed never to be as good as the best Black athletes no matter how hard they practice. But we came to these pages to face truths, not duck them, so let's admit to what is clearly obvious. Black people in general are athletically superior, and the best Black athletes are the best in the world.

Succinct recognition and explanation for this came from Ana Fidelia Quirot, the outstanding Cuban athlete who has set Pan American records in the Pan Am Games in the 400 and 800 meter runs. In a news conference, Quirot (who is Black) was asked by an American journalist why the great majority of exceptional Cuban athletes are Black. She gave an answer that would be considered so controversial as to be forbidden in a society like the United States. (Quote from The New York Times article—Thursday, August 15, 1991) "As you can see, we have no racial discrimination here," (meaning Cuba) she said. "You see on the street familiar relations between Blacks and Whites. I think Blacks do so well in sports because of a congenital ability. It has to do with the genes. The Black race is stronger. It has a better feel for sports. This must be so because Blacks and Whites have the same opportunity to train here."

It is odd and unfortunate that it takes a Black female Communist athlete to elucidate a simple racial truth, which our reputedly open democratic society refuses to face. Obviously the fact that Blacks triumph athletically in a non-racist Communist society where they are neither blocked from other areas, nor better rewarded in athletics—completely demolishes the explanation that Blacks excel in athletics in America for sociological reasons. The real question is, to what lengths will we go—how far will we stretch or suspend truth—in order to ignore that which is clearly obvious? Our academic community has conspicuously ducked and denied the observable racial truth because they fear that admitting Black athletic superiority will set the stage for the awkward counter possibility of White intellectual superiority. But putting on these racial blinders helps no one, least of all the Blacks they are designed to protect. Facing the observable facts does not mean liking them, or subscribing to the foolish and dangerous notion that one race is better than another. Surely we can agree that in the sum total of human talents, and in their worth as human beings, all races are equal. But with this agreement has to come the recognition that the distribution patterns of talents for all races are observably not equal, and trying to subscribe to that fiction only gets in the way of achieving the more even results that everybody wants.

Objectively viewed, Black sports superiority has proven a very useful balancing force in establishing Black stature in America. There is no area where American youths try harder than in sports and to see Blacks prove consistently better in open sports competition automatically forces respect for Blacks at an early age. How can you be better than (or even as good as) someone who beats you fair and square at something where you try your very hardest? Anyone suffering delusions of White supremacy could be quickly cured by setting them up with a pick up basketball game in any Black neighborhood. It would be a crash course in humility that should be prescribed treatment for Ku Klux Klanners. Black superiority in athletics has brought us and taught us new standards of excellence. And for a country that reveres—deifies—sports heroes to the extent that America does, athletic prowess has secured for Blacks a firm position in National prominence, admiration and affection. This is a natural vantage point to be built on—not to be denied because it doesn't fit preconceived doctrines of racial uniformity.

Black distinction in athletics is not the only example of the uneven mix of talents among the races. Based on a lifetime of observation I would have to rate the Jewish people as generally intellectually superior to the general population. From my earliest public school day memories, Jewish students were almost always the smartest in the class. Sure this was partly a cultural thing, family tradition of study, etc. But the results were undeniable. Look at Jewish accomplishments in music, writing, science, medicine, the theater, or Nobel Prizes—in any field where intellectual superiority is required or rewarded—the Jewish people have excelled in numbers that far exceed their percentage of the population. You don't have to be a "Jewish sympathizer" to see this—you have to be a "truth hater" not to see it. Obviously this better mental prowess has been directly linked to better financial success and so Jews, with roughly 2 percent of the population, enjoy more wealth and exert more political influence than Blacks with 12 percent. Unfortunately this kind of accomplishment guarantees resentment born of envy.

In our not yet recognized, but very real struggle to reverse the decline of standards in America, our Jewish community is a key asset, because by and large they have arrived at the achievement level where America needs to go. If all segments of our society performed to the standards of our Jewish citizens, we would not have a balance of payments problem. And despite recent regrettable frictions, the Jewish community is best qualified by example to lead the Black community to where they need to go economically. Because, though unquestionably held back by prejudice, the Jewish people have still moved forward to economic success in America. So they know and can show, the way.

It is strange that these two most visibly talented groups—Jews and Blacks, have also been among the groups most prejudiced against in America—demonstrating among other things the basic irrationality that pervades the whole racial area.

For Blacks the misfortune has been that their slice of racial superiorities does not lie in areas that offer wide, financial opportunity. But the superiorities are there nonetheless. Black leadership in music and entertainment is widely evident. Political accomplishment is now well on its way with President Obama, as is military prominence with the likes of Colin Powell. If it were possible to classify the whole field of charisma and caring as a capacity—yet another area of Black strength emerges. It is hard to imagine anyone galvanizing the national awareness of Aids the way Magic Johnson did. The problem is that these many specific instances of Black superiority in varied areas are not deemed sufficient to compensate for the inherently insulting charge of less mental acuity. Obviously this is not something to be trumpeted in triumphant tones, or even publicly acknowledged, because nobody wants to hear it. It is socially inadmissible evidence. But until we somehow discreetly accept that most Blacks may be economically behind because of real racial differences, we cannot get on with the special remedial programs that are needed to minimize those differences. We see the paradoxical situation whereby liberal thinkers who claim to best represent Black interests, but refuse to recognize racial differences on the grounds of their loyalty to racial equality—have become unconscious obstacles to the practical achievement of that equality. The nettle that must be grasped to get on a productive new course in race relations is that we must begin with an honest recognition of differing racial talents. We can live with that, and work with it—it's the pretense to the contrary that's unmanageable.

For example, is it racial prejudice or simply unwillingness to face relevant facts to observe that those Blacks who seem to have best succeeded intellectually in our society—like President Obama or Colin Powell in their skin tones and features—all observably have some "White" ancestors. Or can we harness these apparently offensive truths and use them, not to denigrate Blacks, but to fashion policies that might work, instead of those that cater to attractive theory at the expense of workable fact?

A national fear of appearing patronizing, or prejudiced is blocking us from the special and separate steps that are needed to bring our Black population up to better levels of prosperity. This has to start early in the schools. Unfortunately, separate and special steps are bound to sound like school segregation all over again. And segregation was once part of the policy of put down and keep down. Nonetheless, I say better some selective programs now with new conscience and purpose—and quality results—than our present policies of de-segregation that observably haven't worked to anybody's benefit, least of all Blacks. There are numerous smart Blacks, and Lord knows, plenty of dumb Whites. There are many individual examples of Black intellectual achievement that individually contradict any theory of racial differences, and there is as much diversity and range of talent in Black ranks as there are in White ranks. But these specifics don't help the general situation because there are palpable differences between the general scholastic abilities of our Black population and the rest of the population. It begins with the difficulties many Black students have learning the same subjects at the same rate and to the same standards as the other races. This is not theory. I went to public school with Blacks and saw it first hand. With the proper corrective programs, Black students will catch up to the other students, far sooner than the other races will ever catch up to Black athletes. Because the gap of superiority between Black athletes and White athletes is far greater than the intellectual gap between other races and Blacks. But the failure to admit either gap, even though they are both obvious to everybody, gets directly in the way of the practical solutions that are the only thing which can alter the inequity. You can walk onto any basketball court and laughingly refer to "the White man's disease" and everybody knows you are referring to the demonstrable inability of Whites to run or jump with anything approaching Black skill or grace. But go into a Physics class and refer to "the Black man's disease" by way of explaining a lack of Black accomplishment in that field and you have probably bought yourself a law suit, or an organized protest. But blinders put on for liberal reasons are just as blinding as those of the less noble variety and they won't get the job of better equality done. At sea, observable truths are the natural postings for determining safe course. It follows that racial policies that begin by asking that we throw out observable truths lose credibility right from the start, and can never end up where they aim to go.

It is of course predictable that this sort of analysis will be greeted by shouts of outrage, howls of anger, and cries of "racist". Professors and politicians will inveigh heavily against any suggestion of inherent racial inequality. The media will activate their finely tuned liberal knee jerk responses, and Black leaders themselves will thunder "foul," making the confusion complete. Lost in all this posturing are the unpalatable facts that have to be acted on for new progress to occur. I didn't invent these facts—I don't even like them, but I do see them.

The announcement, exaggeration or exploitation of racial differences for the purposes of justifying permanently unequal status is clearly wrong. But the recognition of racial differences as a vital first step towards building better equality is a practical necessity because it is only by that recognition that the extra steps that must be taken, will be taken.

Given the aroused sensitivities that surround this subject, it is highly unlikely—indeed impossible for America's political or academic leaders to admit to these realities. In fact they are specifically obliged to publicly deny their existence. Unhappily this only guarantees us a continuation of racial problems that are increasingly corrosive, because ideological dogma forces us to the pretense of denying the racial differences that create the problem.

It may be that the only way to break up this log jam of favored fictions and forbidden truths is for a Black leader of stature to be articulate and forthright on the subject. If "The truth shall set us free," than having a Black leader step forward with an honest exposition of racial realities might set the stage for better results. In so doing, he or she will risk the wrath of the NAACP and other established Black groups. But more importantly, he or she would set a tone of credibility and objectivity that both the Black minority and the White majority could relate to. Policies based on proclaimed equalities that both sides know not to be true, cannot succeed. Elaborate evasions of the truth are in the end more painful than the simple recognition of it. We can live better with the difficult reality of different racial peaks and valleys of talent than with the pretense that they don't exist.

Enduring economic problems with the Black sector of the population is not an American phenomenon—those problems exist in every corner of the globe where there are Black populations, or Black sectors of the population. Since America did not invent this worldwide problem, we do not deserve special blame for it. But, better than any other nation, America is suited to solve the problem, and that is the demanding task at hand.

Seen over the course of my lifetime, our policies and treatment of Black citizens have lurched from early errors of hard heartedness to recent rampages of soft headedness. Nobody wants to go back to the former, but we can sure do with less of the latter.

Though real progress was achieved in removing the legal and attitudinal barriers to Black progress, our additional cure of enforced adjustments—euphemistically labeled "affirmative action" has had the effect of replacing the "old" White prejudice *against* Blacks with a "new" White resentment against Blacks because of policies too plainly prejudiced *for* Blacks. This has meant little net gain in better relations between Blacks and Whites, despite great strides made in opening the way to Black achievement. We have simply added resentment by the White majority to an existing and opposing resentment by the Black minority—creating a larger force of friction that holds back progress.

If we can just step back a bit, and step away from the soothing lather of good intentions, affirmative action can be seen simply for what it is—proficiency welfare—the introduction of counterfeit credits or considerations in order to qualify someone for something that their abilities have not earned. How can such a policy of calculated delusion ever yield competitive excellence? We could try to racially balance the predominantly Black basketball scene by crediting White players with an automatic 5 points, but would that produce better White players?

See how the alleged help of affirmative action has ended up hurtful by generating two strong negatives:

1. It hasn't worked. Decades of propping people up because of their race has not proven to be the jump start able to launch them into eventual equality. Far from being a temporary boost, it has become a permanent crutch, developing dependency where self sufficiency was the need.
2. Affirmative action has created deep resentment, especially amongst White blue collar workers who are taxed to pay *for it*, while at the same time being discriminated against *by it*. Black progress cannot be achieved through White resentment. Let's set aside affirmative action for the non productive artificiality it has proven to be. If Communism and Socialism can come to grips with their failures, and embark on new alternatives—why can't we?

Realistically appraised, a driving national campaign to bring the entire 12 percent of the population that is Black quickly and fully up to the same economic levels as the rest of America on the basis of honest open competition, has about as much chance of succeeding as a quick drive to make the NBA 80 percent White on the basis of honest, open competition. The goals are equally elusive, and for the same intractable reasons of inherent racial differences. Here is where the practical balance of early American philosophy pertains and the rude lessons of the sea instruct.

We cannot achieve what is *socially desirable* by throwing out what is *observably true*. That only results in social and racial policies that "sound good but work bad"—of which we now have an epidemic abundance. The tough design task is to take what is true and steer it steadily towards what is right—without oversteering. Oversteering any ship creates rudder drag, along with erratic course, and the combination impedes true course as surely as it retards proper speed. Smart steering at sea under sail requires using natural forces instead of fighting them. That is a sea lesson America should learn on land.

We are not helped in this challenge by our costly obsession with the unobtainable ideal of equal results. This delusion leads to passing laws of artificial accommodation, which in turn force a slippage of standards, which in turn handicaps America's ability to compete effectively in the world market—thus sapping the one strength necessary to keeping open the ideal of equal opportunity for all races.

There is a great deal in the U.S. Constitution about guaranteeing equal opportunity, but very little at all about guaranteeing equal results. So let's concentrate on the former, and drop the latter as both unobtainable and un-American. We must focus legally and politically on keeping opportunity in America fully open and competitive, which means color blind and free of artificial fixes. With that true measure in place, we can begin in education the tough job of bringing the bottom up, which is not to be confused with our more recent penchant for bringing the top down.

The way forward is clearly shown by the encouraging success of an emerging Black middle class in America. The elements of that success are equally clear—united families with strong family instilled initiatives for education, hard work and self discipline. Not surprisingly these are the same qualities that have taken every other immigrant group to their fair share in America. We don't need to invent new solutions here as much as rediscover the old ones. Painfully it can be seen that a lot of our social engineering on behalf of Blacks has been directly detrimental to precisely those qualities most needed for success. Those exposed to the full brunt of our good intentions have done the worst, and those best able to elude that onslaught of induced dependency have done the best, as our Asian immigrants have convincingly demonstrated.

It is also instructive to review how racial prejudice is handled in the Caribbean, and Latin America. Prejudice exists in those areas just as surely as in the U.S., but the greater racial mixtures tend to diffuse differences and thus defuse tensions. There is not the artificially sharp demarcation between Black and White simply because there are so many tan and brown people walking around, and the resulting ambiance is less abrasive and much more friendly.

Unfortunately, in terms of the social, economic and scholastic scale in the Caribbean, the same pyramid exists with the lighter skinned people on the top, and the darker skinned people on the bottom. Even on the largely Black Caribbean islands, there is a conscious effort by the lighter skinned Blacks to marry amongst themselves. This seems particularly true for lighter skinned women as the preferred choice of darker skinned men, an unfair fashion that lacks intellectual merit and is very tough on "blacker" women. The ability of skin color to subtract reason from the equation is—deplorably—a worldwide phenomenon.

My sense—based on 25 years observation as a resident in Puerto Rico, is that while neither Latin America nor the Caribbean have "solved" racial relations, they definitely "handle" them better. Maybe that is because in more languid, warmer climes, they do not feel so forever compelled to "fix" things by legislative fiat. Nor do they suffer such clearly defined racial power groups. For example, the Black Power Movement was never able to attract support in Puerto Rico—even amongst the "blackest" Puerto Ricans, simply because Puerto Ricans chose to classify themselves as "Latinos". This makes no sense because there is no visible difference between a "Latino" who is Black and an "African American" who is Black. The generally better racial relations in Latin America are also in part due to the greater racial mix between Spanish, Indian and Negro, a mix so pervasive as to defy any attempt at neatly divided categories. So since they can't easily put people in racial boxes—they don't. Latins can even treat the subject of skin tones with humor that is neither intended nor taken to be abusive or degrading. This introduces a kind of saving sanity for which humor is often the catalyst. In America we are both priggish and puritanical in barring racial humor. By insisting on attaching automatic insult to any attempt to lighten racial discussion with a touch of levity, we are again blocking access to balanced truths. This is certainly not a call to bring back tasteless nigger jokes, but rather an attempt to let in a little leavening light.

For example, the efforts of a White population desperately seeking sun tans in order to appear more attractive, while still requiring those born with that same skin tone to list themselves as a separate race, surely deserve to be considered comical. It certainly can't be called rational. In this area where balloons of inconsistency and hypocrisy so abound, we miss the prick of humor. This does not mean that the subject is light or comical, when it is clearly neither. But we need to keep open all paths to the truth, and humor is one of the best avenues available for debunking myths. Persistent myths are the fuel of most racial misunderstandings.

Race relations in America are a confounding puzzle that goes well beyond the status of our Black citizens. But the problems are concentrated there, and the solutions must start there. It is an area in America that most needs fixing. The designer side of me presses for a better design solution, but one can see that the complexities overpower the possibility of any quick fix. Recent racial policies, like affirmative action, have succeeded best in demonstrating ways that work least. New policies need a new pragmatism based on this experience. If there is a new guiding philosophy it should be that race relations will respond better to *reason based compassion* than to *compassion based reason.*

Despite the fact that nowhere in the world do Black people have better opportunity than in the USA—America has long suffered, and often earned, a racist image in the eyes of the world. Regardless of one's political persuasion, the election of Barack Hussein Obama as President has done more to reverse this racist image than any imaginable move. When a Black person can be freely elected—by a White majority—to the highest office in the land, that should put to rest a lot of racist myths. The national outpouring of grief over the death of Whitney Houston is another evidence of a store of affection that goes well beyond her exceptional musical talent. Of course racism still exists in pockets here, and racial tolerance requires continuous effort—but no country has a better claim to racial opportunity than America. The task now is to convert that opportunity to better economic results.

GARRY HOYT

Chapter 4

Fortify English As The #1 Language

(With Spanish A Strong Second)

We have recently seen a rise in the theory that children can be most effectively taught in the language they are most comfortable with, and to some this fact requires multi-lingual public education in the USA. This argument most frequently surfaces in the Hispanic community, a large and growing sector of the populace that has bid strongly for public education in Spanish on the basis of this claim. Here is another area where irrationality perseveres and prospers. The Hispanic category is after all, not a racial but a language category. You can be blonde and blue eyed as a Swede, or copper as a Mayan or black as an African, and if you speak Spanish, or have a Latin name like Gomez or Hernandez, you are automatically classified as "Hispanic". The common denominator of the Spanish language has created a common label for widely diverse peoples— Cubans, Mexicans, Argentines, Panamanians, Dominicans, Puerto Ricans, Venezuelans, Columbians, Peruvians and Chileans. But at the same time this bond of a common language has become their common barrier to full acceptance as Americans. And Spanish has persisted as a speaking preference through generations to a degree not seen with other immigrant languages.

It is as if the Irish, Germans, Swedes, Norwegians, Poles, Czechs, Italians, Hungarians, and French immigrants had all come over here speaking one foreign language, which they insisted on continuing to speak. This one common characteristic might have submerged their various cultural differences, but at the same time it would have mobilized the resentment against them by magnifying the impact of their arrival with a common pivot point for prejudice.

Since I lived in Puerto Rico for many years, traveled widely in Latin America, and speak Spanish fluently, I have some insights to this situation that may be useful. First of all, understand that there are as many differences among Latin Americans as there are among Europeans. But the common Spanish language has forged an automatic cultural kinship among Hispanics that dilutes these differences—particularly when they are bunched together as immigrants in mutually alien territory. The unfortunate other side of the coin is that this common identification badge of language has fueled a wider general prejudice against Hispanics. When you can lump a whole group of immigrants by language under one stereotyped image and label, and call them all Spics or Dagos, it is a lot easier to generate general public mistrust and resentment. Yet how can we ignore a language favored and spoken by almost 20% of our population?

The key fact here is there is no quicker way to inspire widespread mistrust and resentment in America, and to simultaneously postpone your acceptance as full American citizens, than to continue speaking a non English language at the cost of learning English. The issue is not the desirable preservation of Spanish, but the more practical priority of learning and using English. Let's be clear here. Not to learn and use English is an automatic subscription to less earning power and less acceptance in America. Since the cumulative numbers of different people still preferring Spanish are large, and they tend to congregate in separate, cohesive city colonies, prejudice is again facilitated because it is packaged in easily identifiable and concentrated locations. The Hispanic immigrants, particularly the illegal ones, quickly retreat to the better comfort zones of the "barrio" where however grubby the surroundings, they can feel at home because everybody speaks Spanish. Thus the Hispanic immigrants insulate themselves from America with Spanish, and can subsequently also alienate themselves *from* America with Spanish. Nothing separates one group from another as clearly as a different language or a different skin color, and in the case of Hispanics, it is often both barrels at once.

In earlier and less tolerant times, other much smaller groups of immigrants, lacking any such large language sanctuaries to retreat to, were faced with the immediate and complete necessity of learning English. This was not easy, but it was ultimately fair, because the policy was consistent and equally tough for all foreigners. It was, if you will a kind of immigrant's boot camp—not designed for comfort, but very well suited to equip you as soon as possible with the one tool that was indispensable to your economic progress and acceptance as an American—which was speaking English. You literally had no choice but to learn English as quickly as possible—and so you did. I went to public school with many Italians, Greeks and Poles, whose parents spoke little English, but all the children did, because they had to, they were encouraged to— and they became very eager to, because they saw that full acceptance as Americans depended on it.

Consider how our modern sensitivities have disrupted this tough but fair system. Instead of saying "This is America, you must learn English, there is no other way if you want a job and equal respect, We now say "Well of course you want to speak Spanish, you have a right to preserve your Latin culture, and recognizing that we will print your election ballots in Spanish, let you take your driver's test in Spanish, give you full media to entertain you in Spanish, and furthermore teach your children in Spanish at some of our public schools." As a result of this misguided kindness, in the Latin sectors of many American cities it is now possible to be born, live, go to school, be married, have children and die, all in Spanish without ever having to properly learn English. There is of course a high price attached to this kindness—namely permanent poverty and perpetual foreignness to America.

Multi-language education is a system perversely designed to *continue* this imbalance rather than to *correct* it. Thus delusion creeps in again to penalize our treatment of Hispanics, disguised in the same fine raiment of high intentions as our adjustment programs for Blacks. But it is not sensitive, intelligent or fair to postpone the need to learn English, since command of English is critical to economic opportunity and equal respect in America. For Hispanic groups to complain of poor economic opportunity and lack of respect, and at the same time endorse the habit of separate language, is a self inflicted punishment. To the degree that we continue to burden the Hispanic sector of our population with the handicap of non English, or to allow policies that encourage that, we are building an artificially isolated and permanently poor brand of disaffected citizens. In so doing we do not help them, and we certainly don't help America. Being bi-lingual or multi-lingual is an asset to be encouraged, but multi-lingual or bi-lingual education is a snare and a delusion. It creates a separate non accountable teaching bureaucracy, fatally postpones the mastery of English, and by officially sanctioned isolation deprives young Hispanics of their first and best chance to interact with other young Americans.

Again one can anticipate howls and yelps of outrage over this position. Again let's get it straight. Anyone can speak as many languages as they want in America—in fact the more, the better, because languages directly add richness to life. But English is the only language of full citizenship in America, just as French is in France, German is in Germany, Japanese is in Japan and Chinese is in China. The right of Hispanics to continue speaking Spanish is unquestioned, but that should not and cannot become a reason for not learning English—as soon as possible—if you wish to live and work as equals in America. The best way for Hispanics to dispel American prejudice against Hispanics is to remove the handicap of non ability in English, which is the first irritant that fuels the prejudice against them. The primary reason Hispanics have taken longer to enter the mainstream of America than any other immigrant groups is that they have resisted learning English longer than any other immigrant group. And they have been stimulated to this mis-direction by the same liberal theories that profess to be most sensitive to their needs. Regardless of what banner it flies under, the promotion of non English is no favor to any group that wants to make it in America.

True, the learning of English will not by itself solve Hispanic problems. But it will manage the vital first step of raising the linguistic curtain that presently prevents the rest of America from seeing Hispanics as the diverse, talented and gregarious people that they are. You cannot come to America, stay and expect equal station, if you are not willing to unpack your bags to the extent of learning the language of the land. Right away. Ducking, dodging, or deferring that reality only prolongs your status as a perceived foreigner. The burden should not be on America to adjust to the language of the immigrants—but rather should be on the immigrants to adjust to the language of America, which is English.

To appreciate the elementary fairness of this, the exact same advice applies to Americans who might move to Latin America. If they expect to prosper and be treated as equal—better learn Spanish pronto, or in the case of Brazil, Portuguese. Of course if you should go to any Latin land and expect to be able to vote in English, or have your children be taught in English at the public schools—they would be incredulous at your temerity and presumption. Try that in France and the reaction would be complete contempt and scorn. And they would be right. Only in the United States does this kind of divisive foolishness prosper. The idea that it is up to America to teach school in the language of the immigrants who come here is illogical in its assumption, and preposterous in its unworkability.

None of the above has anything to do with trying to force anybody to give up any language they want to speak, or any ethnic customs they choose to follow. That would be undemocratic, unnecessary and undesirable. We are talking about the necessary addition of English—not the subtraction of anything else. The idea that you will lose one language with the acquisition of another is patent nonsense. The rest of the world is busy learning English as a second language—strictly for reasons of practicality since it is the International business language. They do all this with no fear of losing their cultural identity—or displacing their primary language. That we in America should neglect to teach some of our immigrant citizens English while the rest of the world is busy learning it, is folly of the first order.

We can however, take a sensible step that would considerably ease the lot of our large Hispanic population and simultaneously help America. In today's world, everybody should speak at least two languages, and we in America are terribly provincial in our failure to know any language but English. The most logical second language for America to learn is Spanish. Spanish is, after all, the language of Mexico—our large neighbor to the South, and it is (with the exception of Brazil) the language of all of South America. So why not, from the first grade on, make Spanish a required yearly course for all Americans? And really teach it, not just stilted lessons declining verbs—but really learn to speak it, the way most all the European school children today learn to speak English. This would give us an immediate cultural bridge to the rest of our hemisphere, as well as to our own Hispanic citizens. And the young Hispanic kids, struggling at first with English, would have one required subject (Spanish) where they were immediately superior, where their proficiency and ready presence for conversational practice would stimulate the rest of the students to learn quicker, and with the right accents.

Let me dismiss herewith the prevalent notion that Latin American Spanish is somehow not "proper" Spanish. Latin American Spanish is as correct as American English. Mexican Spanish is just as good as Texas English, Argentine Spanish is fully understandable in Madrid, and a Cuban accent is no worse than a Boston one. To suggest or insist on Castilian Spanish in America is like forcing the instruction of Oxford English in America—totally unnecessary and inappropriate.

With this single move of making Spanish a required course for every student, every year from first grade through high school, we would send an important signal of new cordiality to our Latin neighbors— and extend a respectful hand to our Hispanic students by politely learning their language at the same time that we firmly require that they learn ours. Considering the dumb courses we periodically inflict on our public schools (remember the New Math?) setting a new course towards making Spanish an official second language in America would be a beautifully practical move. The same teachers that are presently involved in the mistaken detour of teaching in Spanish to a small group of Hispanics, could be recruited to the larger task of effectively teaching Spanish to all Americans. This would be an "everybody wins" situation. "Ya es hora." It's about time.

We have only to look North to the language cleavage in Canada or to the rapid dissolution of union in the Soviet to observe that national divisions occur almost naturally along the fault lines of different language. There is no quicker way to set up a similar splintering of America, than to undo the cohesive force of the common English language that founded the Nation, and framed all its defining documents.

In the Biblical book of Genesis, it is reported that the construction of a heaven reaching tower in the City of Babel, was interrupted and defeated by the confusion of many different tongues—and the resultant lack of a common one. Making ethnic diversity work in America is tough enough without the addition of a Babel of separate languages to complicate things.

We can see that the proven power of different languages to divide is matched by the equally proven power of one common language to unite. Let us then proceed with that which unites us rather than that which divides us. The primary democratic act of voting requires a common language for nationwide exposition and debate of key issues. The business of doing equitable business requires a common currency of language. And the social acceptance that is the key to everything else depends on the easy daily conversations that only a common language can facilitate.

By all means, let's do a better job of learning other languages, but to make the racial diversity of America work we need the bond of a common language that everybody speaks, reads, writes and understands. Those who would divide us up into contesting camps

35

of different skin color, language, and cultural reference points are creating a nation divisible, where people will have increasing difficulty acting together in the common interest, because there will be ever fewer common interests. So it's English first, and Spanish second, and the sooner we do both—in that order—the better. By way of practical justification, how can we ignore the importance of a language that is employed and enjoyed by almost 20% of our population?

And if you need an example of budding bi-lingual political potential, look no further than Marco Rubio. This young Republican Senator of Cuban extraction is to my mind the most attractive Presidential or Vice-Presidential non candidate, in a Republican Party rather desperately seeking some new star power. Well trained, well spoken and perfectly bi-lingual in English and Spanish, Rubio is uniquely qualified to appeal to the Hispanic share of America. As a successful son of immigrants, he has a story that would favorably resonate with all of America. Could Marco Rubio, like the famous early explorer Marco Polo, be the one to lead to the rediscovery of America?

Chapter 5

Rescue Public Education

I was educated entirely in public schools through high school, and then went on to college and graduate school. In my subsequent business career I had to compete with Frenchmen from the Sorbonne and Englishmen from Oxford, but never did I feel scholastically deprived or penalized by my public school background. Yet my two sons were sent to more expensive, private primary schools, specifically because the more convenient and free local, public schools were plainly deficient in terms of good academic standards. Since both sons went on to attend and graduate from an elite Ivy League college (Brown), I guess I made the right choice. But then I note that all five of my grandchildren were also sent to private schools at considerable expense, which raises the larger question—what happened to create the now widespread inferior standards at the public schools? Isn't Democracy being defeated at the starting line if those who can't afford private schools are forced to accept lower educational value at public schools? And how can America succeed in a global economy if we are delivering a second rate public education to the majority of our young people?

It is instructive to analyze my own personal experience at public high school in 1944-1948. Everybody started out on an equal basis in the homeroom at Plainfield High School—Black, Whites, Hispanics, Italians, Greeks, Jews, etc. But all of us as freshmen had the choice between college preparatory courses, or "commercial courses." This choice was not reflected in your diploma, but it was clearly understood that the college preparatory courses were "harder"—scholastically more demanding, involving chemistry, physics, languages and extensive English, reading and grammar. The "commercial courses" aimed the boys more at shop and mechanic courses, while the girls went more into home economic courses. There was no particular elitism attached to this, and both groups interacted socially and competed equally on school plays, athletics and class officer elections. But if "separate was not equal" an education at Plainfield High School would certainly not be called equal by today's standards.

After my time it didn't take long for research to reveal that there was a conspicuous lack of Black students in the college prep courses. This quickly led to legitimate liberal protests. But the proposed solution of higher Black participation required an immediate "dumbing down" of the college preparatory courses, because maintaining the previous high standards would have resulted in "flunking" a large percentage of students—an unacceptable solution for any public school. So the "White" parents who had counted on a Plainfield High School education to launch their children into good colleges, suddenly found that this was no longer the case. Their only recourse was to find acceptable, and inevitably more expensive, private schools. Thus they were faced with an extensive new expense, while still having to pay the taxes necessary to support a public school system they could no longer use because its standards had been lowered to the point that the kids could no longer get the education base they needed to get into good colleges.

This resulted in a "White flight" out of Plainfield, simply because lower and middle class families could not afford the double expense of private schools, plus the tax burden of public schools that could no longer deliver a proper college preparatory education. The result—when I visited my old high school years after graduation— was that I found an almost entirely Black student body, with armed guards in the halls. The only equality achieved was an even spread of lower quality education—a process of downgrading that did not serve the best interests of anybody—least of all the Black students it was intended to protect.

So in my lifetime I have personally seen public education slip from high quality to a widespread pattern of underachievement. My family experience is very up close and personal, and it covers a wide geographic area that included New York, New Jersey, Pennsylvania, Massachusetts, Rhode Island and Florida. My older brother and I attended public school in N.J. through high school, and from that very satisfactory educational base he went on to graduate from Lehigh and I from Colgate University. Yet we were obliged to send all of our children to private preparatory school at considerable extra expense—strictly because the public school alternatives in their areas were no longer able to deliver a primary education quality that is adequate for entry to the better colleges. This was a very expensive solution, but it did yield good results since our collective 8 children were able to attend and graduate from Brown (2), Princeton, Yale, Pennsylvania, Duke, Mt. Holyoke and Cornell. This fine record is a source of family pride, but it also clearly reveals the tangible decline of the public school system that our taxes paid for, and on which the majority of our citizens have to depend. This is disturbing evidence of a two tier system that contradicts the equal opportunity that America is supposed to represent.

My awareness of public school problems goes even deeper, due to the fact that my wife and sister-in-law both served as public school teachers for a period of 12 years each. Although they both received consistently high evaluations, they were blocked by a rigid seniority system that prevented salary and position progress on the basis of talent. They were in effect driven out by the teacher's union tenure policies, whose unfortunate side effect was often to protect and reward poor and mediocre teachers, while discouraging the better ones. As evidence of teaching talent lost or forced out, my wife became a full time business partner completely in charge of the finances in a successful business of boat design and sales. She also co-designed and supervised the construction of 3 major homes, each currently valued at more than 3 million dollars. Her younger sister, after her teaching career, rose steadily through the ranks to become President and CEO of The New York Times Company, where she served for 7 years with distinction before retiring. So it is clear that training as a teacher can be an excellent preparation for a business career. But it must be equally clear that the seniority based tenure system by which we presently pay and promote our public school teachers, is completely out of step with the basic principle of Free Enterprise, which is to directly reward excellence and penalize failure. Since the quality of the teachers is the vital first step in creating and maintaining better educational results, this dislocation is a costly handicap that we inflict on the general public.

What is more, it makes no common sense in terms of the everyday experiences we all grew up with. How would you like to try to field a baseball team or any athletic team under a system that forced the best young players to permanently wait in line behind the older players already in place? To try to start and run a business on that basis would be a predictable formula for failure.

So we face a dilemma. The best way to make the improvements in public education that America needs to survive and succeed in a global economy is to employ the Free Enterprise incentives that promote the better teachers ahead of the lesser teachers. That way is currently blocked by the Teacher's Union policies of tenure.

It may be that the best way forward is to gradually privatize public education through local PTA control by the parental groups who have the most at stake. To continue the present two tier system in which public schools occupy the lower tier, implies the acceptance of a two level society that is neither fair not smart for America.

Better public education in the primary grades is a basic building block on which our future national levels of accomplishment directly depend. The vital rescue of public education will come only when its excellence is expected and rewarded with the same consistency that its absence is deplored and penalized. There should be no higher priority.

Chapter 6

Resist the Relaxation of Standards

Tests, grades and established standards have long been the triumvirate that measured our lives. All three of these worthies seem lately to have fallen into disrepute amongst those who claim to know best about these things. Tests, we are told, are stressful and unreliable as indexes of ability, because some people don't "test" well. Grades, we are informed, are often elitist in their effect, unnecessarily exaggerating differing abilities and artificially distancing those at the top from those at the bottom. And fixed standards are identified as unfeeling, undesirably rigid measures that don't take into consideration the wide variety of sociological factors that could affect different individual's abilities to meet them.

Well now, this might all be true. But it is equally possible that it is pure bunk, hokum invented by the same lot largely responsible for the steady erosion of dress, manners and behavior in America. In times gone by their efforts might have been labeled "a Communist plot" because there could be no surer way to weaken a country's fiber than to disrupt or destroy the means by which they measure and encourage performance. But it is not a plot, rather it is just a dull degenerative accommodation, which has taken a steady toll of American ability to effectively compete with nations less inclined to hide from the rigors of established standards.

We can start by going back to an historical example, reported by the following news item from The New York Times—November 24, 1985:

"About 200 Black and Hispanic police officers who failed the last examination for promotion to Sergeant will be promoted anyway. Private consultants developed the test in cooperation with the city's police and personnel departments. It was specifically designed to prevent discrimination. Yet only 1.6 percent of the Blacks and 4.4 percent of the Hispanic officers who took the test passed it, as compared with 10.6 percent of the Whites. Associations representing Black and Hispanic officers filed suit asserting that *while the test itself might not have been discriminatory, its impact was.* The city's decision, approved in principle by the plaintiffs, was to promote the 1,041 officers of all races who passed the test, along with the 200 highest scoring Black and Hispanic candidates among the 2,355 officers who failed."

So in the guise of a measure of competence, they are *promoting* a group with the least egregious failures. To see how delusory and self defeating these perversions of true measurement are, turn the situation around. Suppose, at a state track meet, the coach of a small all White team, discovers after time trials that his boys have been shut out of the 100 meter and 200 meter finals, in which all the finalists are Black. (This result is not an invented possibility—it routinely occurs.) He then files suit asserting that "while the trials themselves might not have been discriminatory, their impact was." And so the court decides to let the upper level of the failed White runners qualify, despite the clear evidence that they failed to meet the competitive standard. This example of course sounds ridiculous, and it is—but no less so than the orchestrated adjustments of the police exam. Following those policies will not gain us good runners or good police officers. Hiding performance failures behind allegations of discrimination has become a national reflex, along with our inclination to sue at the drop of a hat to redress any problem. Both these tendencies hurt us, because they encourage the evasion of realities rather than the confronting and solving of them. It is as if we were to go to the doctor, and learning from tests that we had high blood pressure and cholesterol, we should then insist that the tests be changed instead of our behavior. "None love the messenger who brings bad news" noted Sophocles back in 400 B.C. But only fools ignore the message.

Tests are vital because they tell us where you are and you have to know that to know where to go next. Grades are just like the markings on scales, rulers or thermometers, necessary to knowing how well or badly off you are. The prevailing fervor for "pass—fail" grading is a simplistic, fictitious black and white reading of a picture whose real truth lies in its measured gradations, not some arbitrary cleavage that suggests a sharp divide with satisfactory knowledge on one side and unsatisfactory ignorance on the other.

We have lately fallen victim to a tendency that sees in every process of measurement the possibility of some social slight. Instead of reading the plainly obvious results of a test, we are compelled to search out the recondite chance that the results might not in every way be fair, in every instance, to every segment of our population. In which case we are told, the test is unfair and must be discarded in favor of some less candid device that will not offend anyone in any way.

We would do well to recall a pertinent scientific principle known as the "Law of Parsimony." This law, which surfaced sometime in the 14th century states that "you cannot explain a behavioral phenomenon by a higher, more complex process if a lower or simpler one will do." And so when decades of test scores demonstrate that boys tend to do slightly better at mathematics than girls—this is not—as a number of shrill voices would insist—evidence of the sexist nature of math tests. Rather, more plainly, it is simply evidence that boys in general do slightly better at math than girls—just as girls are better than boys at a greater number of other skills.

The time we spend exploring the rather preposterous proposition that numbers are sexist, a contrived complaint requiring a torturous stretching of facts, would be far better spent just accepting this minor instance of male advantage as one of the many disparities of nature that we can very well live with, while we get on to matters more subject to human correction.

Speaking as one to whom high school Algebra is still a painfully recalled, but only dimly understood mystery, I can attest that tests are often neither restful nor reassuring. Squirming in my seat, cursed with a mind that recoiled from fractions and recessed at equations, I could only watch enviously as others around me industriously calculated their way to the correct answers that remained forever elusive to me. I dreaded math tests precisely because I knew they would reveal my weakness. But even in the throes of my dislike for most things mathematical, it never occurred to me to blame the tests for their painfully clear ability to register the scale of my mathematical incompetence.

Rather I simply accepted the useful signal the tests conveyed—that math was something I had to learn, but would probably never be very good at. This realization spared me future embarrassment at the hands of more advanced math and saved my parent's future expense in that direction, enabling me to turn more profitably to things I could do well. Much as I might have liked to blame my mathematical incompetence on some mistreatment of society, or some unfair test—the truth is the tests were just the messenger that brought the bad news. Current efforts to duck or demote tests make about as much sense as recommendations to shoot the messenger who delivers unwelcome news.

We can quibble that no test is completely fair. But that is overlooking the primary utility of tests as necessary positioning, in order to seize upon their secondary flaw of unavoidable imperfection. Better the substantial benefits of imperfect test results than the vacuum of no results, or the deceptive fog of adjusted results.

I recently saw reports of a study which on the basis of preliminary research indicate that children who are breast fed tend to end up slightly smarter than children who are bottle fed. Obviously this is a matter worth pursuing because the implications are important to future decisions that mothers will make. But the comparative measuring point for this research is the I.Q. test, which provides the critically necessary fixed standard by which the intelligence of children raised by both systems can be compared. Almost nobody believes that I.Q. tests are perfect, but how can comparative research like this be conducted without the standard measure of the I.Q. test? There are groups in America who would throw out I. Q. tests because some racial groups consistently do poorly on them. Again—this is shooting the messenger instead of heeding the news. We need to have standards in place as the consistent reference points by which we can ratchet ourselves and society upwards and onwards.

Our pervasively popular tendency to "drop the standards so more will pass" is a self deception that is incompatible with any serious attempt to meet international standards of quality—which will not be "adjusted" for social considerations peculiar to the United States. America must toe a competitive line that is now drawn to world standards, and to do that we must shed the burden of ideological baggage whose net effect is to excuse inferior performance. Those policies were never smart, and they are no longer even kind to those they pretend to defend.

GARRY HOYT

Chapter 7

Enlist The Value Of Military Service

I grew up in the aftermath of World War II when the draft was still in effect. This meant that military service was not a choice but an unavoidable obligation as soon as you turned 17. If you were going to college you were allowed a 4 year postponement, but right after graduation from college your local draft board was immediately on you and you either had to be drafted into the army, or take your choice of enlisting in the Navy, Air Force, Marine Corps or Coast Guard. Many college students took ROTC courses, plus summer training and as a result they were inducted into military service as officers for 3 years right after graduation, rather than serving as drafted Army Privates for 2 years. Another alternative was OCS (Office Candidate School) usually a 90 day after college course that commissioned one to be an officer after completing the course (graduates were known, somewhat with tongue in check—as 90 day wonders). It is fair to say that most of us were not overly enthusiastic about military service, but we were resigned to the legal necessity.

Since my college—Colgate University—only offered ROTC in Air Force—and I was not interested in that, I had to make a choice of another branch of military service right after graduation. I opted for the U.S. Coast Guard OCS, because it was nautical and because the required stay of 2 years was shorter than any other branch. But the Coast Guard OCS programs were all filled up at that point, and the draft board was breathing down my neck for a decision. So the Coast Guard offered me the opportunity to sign up for Boot Camp, with the promise to send me to OCS as soon as the program opened up. As a result, I enlisted in the U.S.C.G. with my enthusiasm well under control. Yet as I look back I have to confess that I probably learned as much or more from my brief stint in the military, as from 4 years in college. This is worth analyzing because we as a nation no longer require military service, and I believe we are the poorer for that omission.

Briefly summarized, my college experience commendably taught me to question things, whereas the initial phase of my military service basically taught me to shut up, salute and take responsibility. It was from the combination of those two very different experiences that the real value emerged. For those who have not served in the military, let me explain.

Consciously or unconsciously, when one goes to college it is an elitist experience—you are dealing with a relatively select group—young people who can pass a number of minimum tests and have the financial means to pay for the privilege of access to higher and wider ideas. In terms of societal perception, and extra knowledge gained, this is a real leg up on those who don't or can't go to college. What college doesn't give you is discipline and exposure to a sample slice of the whole spectrum of the population—which is the reality that you will have to deal with in any post graduate activity. See how military service—starting with the basics of Boot Camp—fills this gap, and provides useful public service along the way.

The Boot Camp experience starts with harsh doses of equality—which initially means even doses of hardship. As one of my fellow draftees noted—"we all get treated the same here—like shit." This uniformity of treatment is accentuated by the required uniformity of dress from head to toe, to haircuts so everybody looks the same. Add to this the fact that everybody rises and retires at the same time, eats the same meals, sees the same training films and is repeatedly obliged to march "in step", for both parade and practical purposes. When marching, anybody who is out of step is immediately noticed and reprimanded by both superior officers and group disapproval. Because the group has to repeat the drill if anybody spoils it by being "out of step". So you learn to stay "in step," as a practical matter of "getting along."

Instead of encouraging and celebrating individuality, as colleges do with individual marks and sports—the Boot Camp experience deliberately and rigorously excises individuality. There is a purpose and a benefit to this because a military group has to learn to act in unison to maximize its effectiveness. Add to this the fact that with enlistment, you are thrown into a diverse group from all walks of life, and you have to learn to get along with them, and to respect their differences—even those that might offend you. Thus Boot Camp was a crash course in the equality of a totally shared experience under totally even circumstances.

In my case, Boot Camp was immediately followed by OCS (Officer Candidate School). This turned out to be a further course in humility since it involved tough courses like navigation and gunnery, which presumed a basic proficiency in math—a subject I had scrupulously avoided since high school. To a man, the rest of my OCS class were graduate engineers who handled the math with aplomb, while I labored intensely and often futilely. Exacerbating this was the rude discovery that they routinely flunked out about one-third of the normal OCS class of 30, which meant you were sent back as a seaman, conspicuously not as an officer. Fortunately at OCS there were also several courses in small boat handling where my experience as a sailor and lifeguard enabled me to shine, so I survived.

When I finally, mercifully, graduated from OCS as an Ensign, my first assignment was to the *Ariadne* an ancient 165 ft. Search and Rescue Cutter based in Key West, Florida. The normal officer compliment was a Lieutenant Commander as skipper (captain) and a Lieutenant as Executive Officer and a crew of roughly 50 assorted Petty Officers and Seamen. Due to some unexpected Officer shortages I was immediately designated Executive Officer, which meant I was placed in charge of navigation, gunnery and ship handling—a very full plate of diverse duties.

I drag you through this somewhat drab history only to point out the dramatic change from my rather carefree student days, to the low level grind of Enlisted Men's Boot Camp, to the concentrated training of OCS, to the rather considerable responsibilities of Executive Officer on the *Ariadne* and occasional service as Commanding Officer of an 83 ft. cutter with a crew of 11. I am not by this suggesting that my assigned duties were exemplary or unique—only that they involved a sudden and serious escalation of responsibility—which is something that military service rather routinely does.

I won't go through the various and numerous experiences involved in Search and Rescue Operations in a small ship in all kinds of weather, but suffice it to say it involved a rapid process of personal maturation that would be impossible to duplicate in a civilian job. I am grateful for that opportunity, and regret that with the departure of the draft and obligatory military service, our young male and female citizens are deprived of that extremely valuable experience. And we as a nation of civilians are not even aware of the loss.

The ironic proof of this was graphically provided, when after my military service and graduate school, I landed my first full time civilian job in New York with Young and Rubicam, a large advertising agency—with the non rank of messenger in the messenger room! In this exalted position, which I shared with several dewy eyed youngsters fresh out of school, I was charged with the awesome responsibility of delivering small packages within the building at 285 Madison Avenue—often with the worried admonition "are you sure you can handle this?" In short I was seriously over qualified and underutilized—not an auspicious start to a business career. But I swallowed pride and adapted quickly and successfully—a minor triumph I credit to my military training.

In addition to what civilians like me learned from the military, there was also a benefit back to the military from the large injection of civilian skepticism they inadvertently received from draftees and "90 day wonders". Since we were not seeking life time careers in the military, we were able to see and question many wasteful and pointless military practices that often got in the way of expeditiously completing the mission at hand. I now read that the military far prefers the present system of volunteer enlistment for the better morale of the inductees, but I worry that while that may produce more harmony, it can also lead to a separate "military" outlook that can stray away from the concerns of the general civilian populace. When, because of the draft, everybody's sons had to bear the risks of war, there was a lot more reluctance to go to war in the first place. That kind of civilian hesitancy might have kept us out of several wars we had no business being in.

What this means is that along with the truth that "War is too important to be left to the generals," is the corollary truism that necessary wars are better waged with strong amounts of civilian participation. That policy automatically brings in outside skills and healthy doses of skepticism about entrenched military practices. My conclusion is that we as a nation would be better off with some required military service—like Switzerland used to have. That would bring the armed forces the unity of a nationally shared experience and equip a lot of our young men with the useful discipline of learning to responsibly shoot off their rifles instead of irresponsibly shooting off their mouths.

Chapter 8

Establish Term Limits and a 50/50 Senate

By way of corrective action, occasionally, but all too infrequently, some brave soul dares to suggest that our National interests might better be served if Congress were invigorated by a requisite infusion of fresh blood and brains. The best guarantee of this common sense benefit would be a Constitutional amendment specifying term limitations—say two 6 year terms for Senators and Congressmen. After all, we limit Presidential terms to two 4 year terms, specifically to avoid the penalties and paralysis of dynastic reign—so why not apply the same sensible precaution to the equally vital role of Congress?

Yet every time this suggestion surfaces it is promptly squelched by a chorus of bewailing voices assuring us that attempts to limit the terms of U.S. Congress "would deprive the country of the skill and experience of its best Public Servants." Well now, certainly no thinking person wants to lose the skill and experience of our best Public Servants. But hang on, isn't that the same group that has given us our staggering National debt, topped off by indiscriminate bailout rescues that were a direct result of Congressional neglect and incompetence? Isn't this the same group that regularly votes themselves generous raises, writes themselves interest free loans, and bounces personal checks at taxpayer expense? If these are examples of invaluable skill and experience, maybe we can better afford to lose them than to keep them.

Certainly by general agreement the recent performances of Congress have not been characterized by either high integrity or intelligence. And these Congress people of questionable intelligence and integrity seem increasingly susceptible to the influence of the lobbyists and pressure groups that surround and beset Washington. Armed with the kind of cash contributions that can influence and control election results, these organized power brokers can now in effect buy and sell Congressmen to favor their causes, and then further protect the durability of their "investments" by working to insure the re-election and permanent presence of their purchased "properties."

This is a tough nut to crack, because by financing the re-election of "their" Senator or Representative, those incumbents are assured of the seniority gains that steadily place them in more important positions on the most pivotal Congressional Committees. This purchased permanence increases their investment value to the lobbyists, and spares the lobbyists the expense of having to "buy" a new set of Congressmen. This purchased and controlled "seniority power" is then merchandized back to voters as the practical means for obtaining special Federal favors for their state or district.

All too passive voter groups are easily swayed to repeated support of incumbents on the grounds that the seniority of their "purchased" Senator or Representative makes them more powerful and better able to deliver pork from the Federal Barrel to state or local interests. No wonder the NRA (National Rifle Association), Philip Morris Inc., and the American Association of Trial Lawyers—three of Washington's most powerful lobbies, firmly oppose term limitations. With the kind of money these power groups have invested in acquiring permanent Congressional pawns that they can control, why would they want to risk losing that control—and have to face the uncertainty of new candidates? Just as the value of a cause is often defined by the character of its opposition, the suspect nature of the above 3 groups ought to prove the merits of the case for term limitation. It's high time.

Other objections raised are laughable in their transparent self interest. We are told we might lose with term limits a lot of the inside knowledge necessary to control the buttons and currents that move Washington. Bravo! Breaking up that cozy network of insider influence is a prime purpose of the exercise. Are we really supposed to believe that the fate of our nation or its future legislative efficiency depends on the perpetual re-election of any one man or woman? Remember that our first President, George Washington, voluntarily stepped down, resisting those who wanted to make him a King, and wisely noting that turnover was necessary and desirable in democratic government.

History and Shakespeare teach us that "all power corrupts and absolute power corrupts absolutely." It follows that the more reliably we can periodically disperse our political power center in Washington—the better off we will be. We do it with Presidential term limits, why not with Congress? At the very least, Term Limitations would insure a periodic flushing out of rascals before they can become too firmly entrenched. And at the very best, term limits would open up Washington to a guaranteed influx of new people and new ideas. Yes, we will lose the good services of some good people. But we will also gain reliable protection against the ossified thinking of politicians whose prime time has passed, who are kept in place by the combination of public indifference, plus the financial pressure of groups whose influence can too conveniently be funneled to the incumbents.

What we need in Congress, and what Term Limits would induce are 3 new types of legislators.

1. An influx of younger people who are aware that they will be obliged to return to earning a living in the outside world after their Congressional service. Not the Washington world but the real world where you actually have to make something more than meetings and grow something more then deficits. An active awareness of their future as regular citizens might shape Congressional actions to be more in tune with the realities the rest of us are forced to live with. And by eliminating the need for a lifetime commitment to politics, we open up the prospect of a brief political career to a much wider group who could justify limited duty, knowing they will be going back to other careers. Thus they would bring fresh thinking and more youthful energy to public life and bring back that public service knowledge to their private citizen lives, along with a strong realization that they will be required

to make their future living under the laws they pass during their time in Congress. This is a sobering consequence that is missing in our present set up of nurturing lifetime politicians.

2. Bringing in an older group seasoned by the experiences of having earned a living, raised some kids, and made their way in the world, would inject that practical perspective into a twilight career in Congress. The hard earned workplace experience of what it takes to survive and prosper in the outside world might curtail some of the counter productive measures that periodically seem to sprout up in Washington. Enabling more senior citizens to cap their business careers with public service would gain their service at a time in life when they might want to give something back—rather than take something out. Let's get in place in government some people with a time tested grasp of the economic realities that we would like to see government either stimulate or get out of the way of.

3. Along with Term Limits, institute a move to insure the more equal representation of *women* in Congress. The present largely male U.S. Senate is an anachronistic under representation of those who make up more then 50% of the population. We freely concede that the best managed families require 50/50 male/female participation and that single parent upbringing often critically lacks the vital input of the other sex. So why wouldn't our government equally benefit from that same better balanced formula? Why shouldn't the Senate be composed of one female Senator and one male Senator from each state? This would seem to be a practical adjustment to achieve the kind of fully representative body that Congress is intended to be. This would need a Constitutional amendment to ensure the higher female participation in the Senate that a proper representation of the population requires. And in so doing America would gain the benefit of new perspectives from a neglected source of wisdom.

Does anyone seriously doubt that we receive vital separate knowledge from our Mothers—at least equal and in many cases superior to Fatherly advice? Is it not logical to expect that adding feminine yin to masculine yang would yield new wisdom and a balance that is too often absent from Congressional action?

I see the combination of term limitation and a 50/50 male/female Senate as a key to revitalizing the U.S. Congress. We should eliminate from the Washington scene the predominantly male lifetime politicians. We have had too many of those, and they have proven too prone to foolish wars, overly partisan politics and a costly preoccupation with re-election.

Chapter 9

Beware the Perils of Religious Extremism

Religious Freedom is a value that drew many of the first settlers to America. As such it deserves and receives protection under the U.S. Constitution. But there are instances where this freedom escalates for some into zealotry—a certainty that *their* way, is *the* way. This can translate quickly to intolerance that justifies actions and intrusions to force others to conform. Fortunately there is enough congruity in the religious beliefs of Catholics, Protestants and Jews so that open abrasions are minimal, and that fact enables Freedom of Religion to be an agreed upon positive force of tolerance in America, rather than the divisive source of frictions that infect areas like the Mid East.

What has interrupted the tranquility of this intellectual truce has been the emergent threat of Muslim intolerance. In an ironic twist, where Marxism called for the relatively mild course of bypassing religion as "an opiate of the people," Islam calls for the active, forcible eradication of other religions in order to forcibly impose their own. This is about as far from religious freedom as you can get. The frequently demonstrated willingness of Muslim militants to blow themselves and others up is evidence of how quickly religious extremism can translate to fanatical violence. Seen in this light, 9/11 was as much a declaration of war against the United States as Pearl Harbor was.

Reason cannot reach nor kindness soften, the hard wired hatred of the religious fanatics who are all too often created and tolerated by the Muslim religion. The monstrous illogic of the Madrassa fueled concept that all non Muslims deserve death for their non belief is an active, present day menace that leaves little room for sensitive tolerance or civilized debate. Consider the statement of the "underwear bomber", who at his sentencing asserted that Muslims were "Prepared to kill in the name of God, and that is what God told us to do in the Koran." (NYT, Feb. 17, 2012)

One can accept the fact that not all Muslims are terrorists, but that does not explain or excuse the fact—confirmed by 9/11—that most modern terrorists *are Muslims.* The sobering new reality is that there is a strong worldwide religion out there—sections of which would—if they had the power—just eliminate the Western World, starting with Israel. Armed with the certainty of religious extremism, the low tech, highly motivated individual suicide bomber becomes the ultimate guided missile that no sophisticated defense system can fully protect against.

This is not a situation that lends itself to calm contemplation or patient reasoning—the tools normally expected in debating civilized solutions. When a large group has repeatedly pledged your destruction and apparently awaits only the gathering of sufficient power to do so, they have to be treated not as democratic opposition, but as the active enemy they repeatedly profess to be.

It is instructive to observe the Israeli reaction to all this. As the designated first target, Israel knows they cannot rely on a strategy of prompt retaliation because given their small size, accepting a first nuclear strike could be terminal. Even America's supporting pledge of prompt retaliation to any attack on Israel is small comfort if accepting the first nuclear punch for them means accepting oblivion. *The assured retaliatory destruction of one's enemy is no satisfaction, if your own destruction has to precede it.*

This issue raises perplexing questions. For example, our much valued "Freedom of Speech" quite sensibly does not allow anyone the right to shout "fire" in a crowded theater. Nor is anybody or party allowed the right to advocate the violent overthrow of the U.S. government. Because in its logical extension that could mean utilizing the "Freedom of Speech" in order to eliminate it. What sense then does it make to allow the benefits of Freedom of Religion to extend to a religion that openly proposes to eliminate the Freedom of other religions as soon as they are able to. Of course this seems a remote consideration, given our constitutionally protected separation of Church and State and the current, relatively small size of the Muslim religion in the U.S.A. But there is enough recent evidence of home grown Muslim terrorists to warrant new concern.

When Religious certainty calls for the elimination of all "non believers" and awaits only the collection and opportunity of sufficient power to do so, they cannot be treated as "just another religion". They are so committed to being a future foe, that they should be treated as a current foe.

The plain fact is that Muslims had nothing to do with the original founding of America or with forging the democratic provisions of the U.S. Constitution. And while they are anxious to operate under protection of our Freedom of Religion, the dictates of their own Muslim religion would require the elimination of those Freedoms for others as soon as they have the power to do so.

At sea this would be like allowing aboard new crew members who are pledged to mutiny as soon as circumstances allow. The Muslim religion, by its own repeated principles and performance is intrinsically intolerant of other religions, and in the case of Israel is actively pledged to their eradication. This aggressive philosophy exemplifies the dangers of religious extremism, and nautical caution requires new watchfulness on these clear storm warnings.

GARRY HOYT

Chapter 10

Cultivation of the Mind's Eye

Let's begin by recognizing that the many wonderful things you can do *with* the computer are matched—and often exceeded by—the many wonderful things you can do *without* the computer. Doubters can verify this by checking out the drawings of DaVinci, the sculptures of Michaelangelo, the writings of Shakespeare and the music of Mozart. Today one looks with concern at the way increasing numbers of young Americans are mesmerized—transfixed—by small hand held electronic devices, often to the neglect of the deeper promise of printed pages. My theory is that this has to do with a regrettable neglect of "the mind's eye"—that magical faculty by which we are able to convert a written or verbal description—or even a passing thought—into a very clear mental picture. In today's world, where everything tends to be "shown us" by screen, I fear we are losing, by atrophy, this vital skill of visualizing. It is a mistake to think that visualizing yields a less clear picture than the computer screen. When I read Robin Hood as a young boy—I did not need to think of Kevin Costner's screen portrayal, because my mind's eye had already delivered to me a very clear picture of Robin, Maid Marian, and Sherwood Forest, complete with more intense color and more dramatic action than any movie. Without arguing the obvious modern indispensability of the computer, it remains equally necessary to develop the keener perceptions of the mind's eye, which enable you to see an object—in action—even before it exists.

Of course the next stop in visualizing a design idea is to be able to sketch it. This is where the natural interaction between book reading, cursive writing and free hand drawing starts to emerge. That does not mean you have to be an artist, but developing the manual skill of drawing can definitely help the creative process. And cursive writing is better training for this than typing because it directly involves the management of curved letter shapes. The way we learned in grade school by copying the teacher at the blackboard. It's too bad that for too many people, cursive writing has degenerated into illegible scrawls. It is instructive to remember that all our defining documents—Declaration of Independence, Constitution and Bill of Rights were originally rendered in hand script—demonstrating the close tactile relationship between conceiving important thoughts and presenting them convincingly in graceful cursive writing. Sadly this is a skill that is apparently now being phased out at many of our preparatory schools because it is judged to be old fashioned and "not computer friendly". What, one asks, is then to become of the cordial "Thank You" note or the passionate love letter? These are things that for their full effect, require the personal touch that only hand writing can deliver. This is a skill that should not be allowed to slip into obsolescence.

Getting back to books, consider how—more than any other instructional process, book reading is personal and patient. In books the wisdom of the ages is neatly packaged for your private perusal—in your home, at the library or lounging on a beach. Reading a book allows you to analyze and absorb at your own pace, going back to remove doubt, and marking for later retrieval those passages that interest you most. A well written book remains a personal arsenal of words shaped and organized to useful purpose, a clever companion ever ready to delight, console, or inform. Comfortably seated by a blazing fire, with a glass of pleasing red in hand, a book becomes your passport and transport to wide selections of adventure or tranquility. And yes, there *are* special rewards for book reading aboard a well found sailing ship, safely anchored in a snug harbor on a stormy night. Because a sailing vessel at rest is a potential exploration at hand, awaiting the stimulus that a good book plus the mind's eye can uniquely provide.

Chapter 11

The National Need for Common Denominators

Common denominator experiences are those formative events in our lives that are widely enough shared throughout the nation so that the citing of them creates an instant bond of mutual understanding.

Seen from the vantage point of my 80 years, the two most defining common denominator experiences in my life have been—first—public school education and—second—military service. Both of these are discussed in separate chapters of this book, but I restate them together here for their important conjunctive impact—emphasized by the way one closely followed the other. I see a sad subtraction of those factors in today's America, and that decline pinches our national enthusiasm and resolve. I should point out that in my case both public school and military service were unavoidable obligations, not voluntary choices, so I can claim no credit for their selection.

Let me explain. My father was a gifted but financially troubled cartoonist, whose chronic lack of income made public school a practical necessity. Yet my early years could not in any way be described as hardship, because my dear mother's well to do parents had presented her—as wedding gifts—with two mortgage free homes in fashionable neighborhoods—one for summer at the shore and one for winter residence. This meant growing up with the curious bifocal view of having some of the accoutrements of wealth, without the monetary actuality of wealth. In those days (1940-1948) public school education did not carry the learning deficit it has now deplorably acquired. Furthermore, back then public schools had some specific advantages over private schools, which tended to be smaller, all male or all female enclaves. In contrast the numerically larger public schools offered a much more balanced mix, which jointly involved boys and girls from all walks of life, along with generally better athletic programs. This was a significant benefit that I only recognized later in life.

As previously described, public schools back then required a choice between the more difficult college preparatory courses and the less scholastically rigorous, but more practical commercial courses. This in effect created a two level public school education system that was more expedient, but less egalitarian. Of course it didn't take long for liberal elements to discover this discrepancy, which they promptly solved by imposing the dreary solution of one level with lower educational standards. That immediately resulted in a "White flight" out of public schools into the private schools who maintained the higher standards necessary to get into good colleges, leaving the public schools in the lurch of lesser standards. We complain about having a divided nation, but part of this division can be traced to the difference in quality between our private and public schools.

Equally costly was the subsequent loss of an early on, across the board sampling of the diversity of America—a common denominator benefit that public schools provided much more effectively than the restrictive lenses of private schools. For example, racial snobbery did not prosper in public schools, particularly among young males where a scale of physical superiorities immediately established its own meritocracy. In this teenage male world being stronger definitely outweighed being smarter—and anyone questioning that was quickly neutralized by a punch in the mouth or a bloody nose, usually delivered by the Black kids or Italian kids who were observably "tougher" than their "White" counterparts. Since I was always the youngest and usually the smallest White guy in my class, these realities were very graphically demonstrated to me. At that time I was not always grateful for these lessons, but in the reflections of later years I can see their value. You simply had to learn to adjust to new realities, a process that was much more useful than complaining about their lack of fairness.

By the same token, the principal benefit of obligatory military service was not in its training for war, but rather in its value as a common denominator experience that everybody had to share. This shared endurance and acceptance of what was essentially a considerable personal inconvenience became an integral element in shaping the national character and identity that every nation needs for distinction. Unity is automatically created when everybody has to do the same thing, a common experience that neither wealth nor privilege can buy your way out of.

Unfortunately it seems to take the undesirable urgency of war to create any national willingness for obligatory military service. So the formation of the next "greatest generation" may depend on the arrival of cataclysmic events that nobody wants to happen. But one way or another we need to combine the opportunity of higher scholastic standards at public schools with the useful lessons of duty and discipline, which are well taught by military service.

I can attest that the young males who currently cause most of our crime problems would be the first to benefit from the discipline of obligatory military service, and the nation as a whole would gain a presently missing sense of national purpose. The problem is that the current politicians who control all this are simply unaware of the benefits of what they have not personally experienced, so the strong likelihood is that those who can afford it will continue to gain a better education in private schools, while the general public languishes in the less challenging ambiance of mediocre or poor public schools. And military service will be delegated and relegated to a small group of professional volunteers. I gather that the various directors of our military forces would prefer to deal with willing volunteers as opposed to reluctant draftees. But just as the general public would benefit from exposure to military service, so too would the military benefit from regular injections of civilian skepticism. And there would be far less willingness for America to enter into foolish wars if every family knew there was a chance their own sons or daughters might be called into active service and danger.

In short, the decline of public schools, and the absence of brief obligatory military service will probably continue to deny us the valuable common denominator experiences we need as a nation to marshal our diversity into the unity of feeling and acting like one people. We are the poorer for this subtraction.

Chapter 12

The Unity of Common Purpose

This is the element most critically lacking in America today. It is an element we don't have to invent, because there was a time in World War II when we once very clearly had it. I am well qualified by age to report on this, because as a boy of 10 in 1941 I was a first hand witness to that time when America came together in ways that would be almost unimaginable today.

In WWII Americans of all ages, races and geographic locations bonded quickly, firmly and publicly together with no discernible dissent. All eyes were firmly fixed on the goal of defeating the Axis power of Germany, Italy and Japan, and all resources were committed completely to that end. The Axis powers had the claimed strength of greater national homogeneity and this *Aryan* purity did form formidable national units of similar racial characteristics. But that proved, in the fierce contest that ensued, to be not as strong as America's composite strength of differing racial talents bound together with the unity of common purpose.

There are important lessons here. Without common purpose, racial diversity becomes merely a distracting fragmentation that weakens national effort. But with the unity of common purpose the separate strands of differing tastes and abilities can be woven together to form a synthesis of greater strength. America was the first major nation in history to accomplish this. And the momentum forged by American unity in WWII carried through to create the world's foremost economic and military power in the following years.

What is perhaps more notable, this period of American dominance was capped by a postwar *reticence of power* that was also historically without precedent. What other nation, victorious and armed with the might of exclusive, invincible atomic bomb power, would simply disarm quickly and send its triumphant troops home without any territorial expansion? All America claimed was enough land to bury its dead. And what other nation, when faced with the unexpected and extensive postwar expansion of Russian communism, would opt for the non violent strategy of simply luring the opposition into an armament race they couldn't afford? We don't get or take enough credit for this admirable restraint. This again set an historical precedent whereby American Capitalism eventually vanquished Soviet Communism without firing a shot.

There are some relevant sports parallels to these major political issues. For example, football is the quintessential American sport. And it became so because it fuses widely different physical skills, and mobilizes them in ways that are totally different from other sports. Consider the widely different sizes and weights of the players, which can range from Wes Welker's 175 pounds to Patriot teammate Brian Wilfork's massive 300 pounds. Then consider the unique structure of the game, which is composed of programmed pauses (huddles) that plan and pace the action, with separate action attempts (downs), which can be carried out in either a prolonged drive consisting of small incremental yardage gains, or single strokes of long runs or passes for large gains. In football, each team has a game plan for each game, which is carefully developed based on one team's array of speed, skill and power, versus the opposing team's array of speed, skill and power. The game is played regardless of the weather and in its philosophy and execution—American football is a microcosm of American business practices. Football teams from Pee Wee to High School, to College are prime examples of the teamwork created by the unity of common purpose. Virtually every schoolboy and schoolgirl grows up with a close awareness of how football can mobilize regional spirits and efforts around local teams. On any Saturday afternoon during football season you can walk into any small town in America and you will find most of the town gathered enthusiastically at the local football field (that every town has) watching the local high school football teams play. This is a uniquely American phenomenon, and worthy of note for that reason alone.

The national passion for football extends well into the professional game. The recent 2012 Super Bowl game attracted 111 million viewers—the largest single TV audience ever assembled in America. Unfortunately this strongly shared national enthusiasm does not extend to civic affairs—where the sad reality is that today we seem to be living less in "the United States of America", than in "the divided states of America". The media constantly bombards us with reminders of how the privileged 1% of our population is exploiting the abused 99% of the population. This kind of divisive class warfare is leading us nowhere except to despair, with its unfortunate recourse to ever bigger government remedies.

As the title of this book suggests, we need to *Rediscover America*. Part of that task could be described as just better housekeeping, but beyond that we need an overarching reclaim of the pioneer spirit that used to animate American efforts. Maybe it's because I watch too many late evening Westerns on TV, but I still feel we can recapture the strength of that simple story line whereby virtue is rewarded and the good guys win. I guess that admission reveals me as a conservative, but you probably figured that out already. I hope these ramblings may prompt useful discussions, and remind you that some of the best perspectives on common purpose can be found at sea, under sail.

Chapter 13

Serving A Wider Spectrum of Excellence

Back in the days before television numbed our brains with repeated assaults of violence and bad taste, young people actually studied to learn how to read and write. This was a process that involved a number of somewhat tedious drills, along with dull routines of memorizing correct spelling, learning grammar and sentence structure. Back then we were also obliged—prior to any actual writing—to learn to prepare "outlines" of the subject to be covered. The theory, quaint by today's standards, was to first make a "forecast" of the ideas to be presented, in order to better organize flow and presentation. Orderly, sequential thought has since fallen into disfavor, as alien to today's culture as pleasing melody and coherent lyrics are to the cacophony of rap. It is conceivable that this lapse is not entirely unrelated to the distemper of the times. For the sake of nostalgia and old time verities, let me outline five things America needs to address:

1. Competitive productivity
2. Clean environment
3. Better public education
4. Political integrity
5. Public safety, tranquility and social harmony

Surely we can agree that it would be a fine and wondrous thing if America could improve in all these areas, and indeed our politicians regularly promise to do so. The problem is that instead of moving steadily ahead, we are—under their direction—falling steadily behind. My thesis is that it is not America's proscribed destiny to fall behind, and that we can stop doing so by paying better attention to new International markers, and some old American ones. What we have experienced in recent years is a severe leakage of standards out, followed by a matching flow of bilge water in. This has caused our otherwise excellent Ship of State to pitch, wallow and broach in a manner not conducive to forward motion. This suggests that we abandon, not the ship, but those things that have come to menace the ship, which could be capsulated as strife, license, and the pursuit of foolishness in the name of fairness.

We now see a lee shore littered with the flotsam and jetsam of economies lured aground by the siren song of Socialism. Yet despite this consistent record of wreckage, there are still those who bow to its captious theories, or modified versions thereof. Forever wringing their hands over freedom's failure to provide equally to everybody, they are forever blind to Socialism's remorseless inability to provide adequately to anybody. Diluted doses of this dilapidated economic theory may not be instantly fatal, but in prolonged application they are ultimately lethal. Even countries like Sweden, equipped with rich natural resources, a developed economy and a small highly educated homogeneous population find their vitality steadily eroded by the subtractions of Socialism. We must engrave those lessons in our national memory, lest we drift down the same false channel.

A high salute should go to Russians like *Sakarov* who manned beleaguered turrets of truth in the face of overwhelming collectivist pressure. Caught in the maelstrom, they refused to be swept away, and we owe much to their courage to stand fast. While academics comfortable in the west were mouthing fashionable assent, he and others chose dangerous dissent. And even after suffering the withering cruelties of imprisonment in the Gulag, their first actions on release were to stand up and reaffirm the same democratic rights that got them put away. We are indebted to these pioneers of courage. We need American leaders with similar resolution and intellectual clarity to resist the drift to ever bigger government solutions.

In my lifetime, the greatest crimes against society have come from those doctrines promising the greatest good for society. Stalin killed 20 million of his own people under the pretense of delivering social justice. This does not mean we should ban do-gooders, but it does suggest we should keep a wary weather eye on those ships which fly social justice as a flag of convenience. I draw your attention to Hoyt's first law. "All that is necessary to convert laudable intent to lamentable result is control by a government agency." Yet that truth has to be seasoned with the crisis need for government action when business greed and stupidity combine to corrupt the natural efficiency of free enterprise. The point here is not to let occasional corrective disciplines become the kind of operating norm that will strangle entrepreneurial effort.

The new role for American business is to recognize that better education, cleaner environment, and social harmony are not just esoteric goals, but evidence of the new wider spectrum of excellence that must be served by enlightened enterprise. Business decisions that do not meet these new criteria are wrong, regardless of their other merits. Getting into these new channels, unfamiliar waters to business, will require new steering skills. None of this means abandoning the profit motive which will continue to be indispensable to stimulate the individual incentive that is key to free enterprise. But profit cannot be allowed to trump principle, because it is the preservation of principles that protects the open playing field that free enterprise needs above all.

I see a particular opportunity here for encouraging and rewarding America's emerging corps of female executives. This is an area where we are still lagging behind. Once we get past the foolishness of having women trying to act the same as men in order to prove they are as good as men, we can break through to the more productive ground where women are free to act as women—giving us the gain of that different perspective that America needs. It can be seen that women's greater emotional sensitivity, far from being some imagined business weakness, is more accurately seen as a special strength in managing the new wider spectrum of excellence that will face tomorrow's businesses. We should consider requiring corporations to include in their annual reports specific reporting on positive contributions to matters like clean environment that affect everyone.

This is not to be confused with some starry eyed social agenda. Hoyt's second law is, "Social policies that lead to economic inefficiency automatically handicap their own validity." It is in the balanced integration of social goals that new business distinction lies. It would not be surprising to see women executives manage this balance better than men. To these new helmspersons I can't resist some parting and undoubtedly repetitious advice from an old sailor. To wit: Hoyt's third and final law, "A free enterprise society is the only one capable of creating enough wealth to accommodate the problems of its better distribution." Keeping the competition free and open takes some doing, since people are forever trying to make it come out even, which it can never be. Given the observable truth of differing human talents, there is no sense to the expectation, and certainly not the enforcement, of uniform results. Equal opportunity plus the free exercise of differing abilities is always going to yield unequal results. That is not social injustice at work, it is reality at work. The trick is to steer a course between conservative hard heartedness and liberal soft headedness. That safe and sane middle course is never precisely defined, but it is well marked by a careful avoidance of the bordering extreme solutions, and remember that, "Creating policies of artificial preference will not solve problems of prejudice—because artificial preferences are what prejudice is." Maybe that is the fourth law.

For our future guidance, a good model of successful innovation might be the American clipper ship, which in its day led the world in bold explorative endeavor. Built entirely in America from the keel up with native materials, they were technological marvels of their time, designed by the best designers, built by the best craftsmen and sailed by the best seamen. In their design, construction and operation, the clipper ships epitomized purposeful propulsion to rewarding destinations. All persons aboard had a functional relation to the faster and safer handling of the ship. (Lacking the requisite connection to useful purpose, lawyers, and stock brokers were left ashore.) The pay of captain and crew was directly dependent on the successful completion of the voyage and the pay grades of the crew were reasonably related to the skills involved. Together they set tall sails, risked uncharted waters, feared no foreign competition, and welcomed open trade. Modern recall of these simple principles would be an excellent start towards reclaiming the lead for American enterprise.

We need to rediscover and give right of way to those priorities that lead to propulsion forward, as opposed to those that drag us back with divisive departures from the free enterprise practices that made America the world leader. The legitimate needs of minority groups can never be properly addressed when those concerns are allowed to disrupt or subvert America's ability to compete effectively in the international economic arena—because now it will be our success there, on which all else depends.

Those who put fairness first must not allow their commendable zeal to obscure the reality that any sustained fairness depends directly on sustained economic success. From that axiom springs the corollary truth that the fairest societies are not necessarily those who most vocally proclaim it, but those whose economic success best allows fairness to consistently blossom. Fairness should be a priority result of economic efficiency, but the economic ship must first sail fast and well to have any hope of offering passengers and cargo better safety, comfort and prompt arrival.

Serving this new spectrum of excellence calls for the diversity of many colors in the crew, but the star they must together steer for is a newly resplendent American exceptionalism whose luminescence is universally seen as guide worthy. America cannot police the world or provide for the world, but by steering a proper course we can effectively lead by productive example. Historically, America's most defining characteristic has been the liberation of the individual's resources via free enterprise. That is the homeport to which we must return, reaffirming the ascendant notion that people should be responsible for their own actions, and thereby serve their own society and the world. Since I am limited by advanced age, you dear reader have the helm for that challenge. So point up—don't pinch—check the lay line—and mind you don't overstand the mark.

Deciphering that advice requires a smattering of nautical knowledge that would benefit anyone. And what better way to acquire that knowledge than via the simple process of learning to sail—something which precocious 8 year olds routinely manage. Sailing deftly demonstrates how natural power can be harnessed to pleasurable purpose. That useful lesson illustrates how the most ancient medium of discovery can help serve the modern cause of Rediscovering America. Sail ho!

About The Author

Garry Hoyt is a yacht designer, artist and writer, currently residing in Newport, RI. He is the author of four books, Go For The Gold, Ready About, Go For The Green and Isla Verde, as well as numerous articles in marine magazines. In 1976 Hoyt founded Freedom Yachts, which pioneered ocean going boats with free standing spars. He was an Olympic sailor in the Finn Class, placed third in the Snipe Worlds and won the Sunfish World Championship in 1970, along with a wide variety of sailing titles in the Caribbean and the U.S. In January 2000 he was named by Sail magazine as one of the most influential sailors of the past 30 years.

In his earlier career in International advertising, Hoyt lived for 25 years in San Juan, Puerto Rico, where his two sons were born. During this period he traveled extensively to Latin America and the Far East as Area Manager for Young & Rubicam, plus Managerial Director of Y&R offices in San Francisco and Chicago. This experience plus his knowledge of Spanish has given him an informed view to the interconnected worlds of Latin and American politics. This is the unique perspective that he brings to *Rediscovering America.*

A 1952 graduate of Colgate University, where he majored in English Literature, Hoyt also received a graduate degree from The Thunderbird School of International Management. He served as a Lieutenant J.G. in the U.S. Coast Guard with Search and rescue duties in Florida and the Caribbean.

Available at www.amazon.com and other retailers.

www.garryhoyt.com